Call o

For Tony, my selkie son

BL- 5.1
AR pts.
3.0

Contents

Chapter 1 — 5

Chapter 2 — 16

Chapter 3 — 28

Chapter 4 — 38

Chapter 5 — 54

Chapter 6 — 66

Chapter 7 — 81

Chapter 8 — 89

Chapter 9 — 103

Chapter 10 — 115

Appendix – Selkie Spellings — 125

Chapter 1

"Go away," said Ryan. He stood on the shore, arms folded, his body a barrier between the headland behind him and the girl in front of him.

"Why can't I go with you?" Cilla sounded hurt and puzzled.

"I want to be by myself," said Ryan.

"What's the problem?"

"I just need a little time to think," said Ryan, "on my own."

Cilla tossed her head, and her hair lifted in the breeze. "Suit yourself," she said and turned away.

Ryan sighed with relief and began climbing the rocks. He and Cilla had been friends since her family came to the beach town two years ago. Cilla's family had moved into the house just across the road. Ryan had been glad to have someone his own age in the small community of mostly retired people. He hated sending Cilla away, but he couldn't risk her seeing what was at the bay. She was hopeless at trying to keep secrets.

He pulled himself up the jagged rocks. Skinned knuckles and shins had taught him which handholds and rocks to trust with his weight. He made his way over the headland, toward the hidden access he had discovered a few months ago.

Ryan glanced back to make sure Cilla wasn't following him, then he leaped off the rocks onto a small half-circle of sand wedged between the headland and a cliff face. It looked as if he could go no farther.

He turned to a large boulder jutting out from the sheer cliff; it seemed to be welded into the cliff face itself. He scaled the rock and slid over the top. A gap between the side of the boulder and the cliff led to a narrow tunnel.

Dropping to his knees, Ryan wriggled through the opening. It took several seconds for his eyes to become accustomed to the dark cavern, then he moved ahead. Around a bend in the tunnel, a glimmer of light lit up his path.

As he scrambled toward the exit, he thought of the day in early summer when he had fled to the sanctuary of the bay. Sheltered from the fierce coastal winds, the bay was a haven from the many storms at home.

Ryan didn't know exactly why his parents would start fighting, but the angry words and slammed doors always made him feel sick to his stomach. He would shut himself in his room, turn up the volume on his stereo, and play his harmonica to block out the raised voices. But the animosity filling the house still suffocated him.

One day, when he heard his parents start in again, he left the house and headed for the bay. After emerging from the tunnel, he was buffeted by wind squalls as he slid down the steep bank, toward the rocks. Spray from the ocean mingled with the tears on his face.

A bellow coming from beyond the rocky point startled him. It started as a deep roar and ended with a harsh bark like a dog being strangled. The bellow rang out again. It must be a large animal to make that much racket, Ryan thought.

Ryan clambered around the point and stopped. On the far side of the bay, a female fur seal lay in the shelter of some rocks. Her body shuddered and swayed as she raised her head, swinging it from side to side.

Unwilling to provoke or disturb the creature, Ryan crouched beside a large boulder. He watched as the seal heaved herself upright and supported her body weight on her front flippers. She seemed to be in distress.

She flapped and whacked her splayed hind flippers on a flat rock. Ripples spread down the sleek length of her body. Her huge dark eyes bulged and spiky whiskers drooped from beneath her nose.

Ryan squinted as a dark, shiny lump slid from beneath the seal's tail flippers. The animal groaned and hitched itself forward, shedding more of the glistening mass. The steaming bundle flopped onto the rock, lay still for a moment, then twitched.

The seal gave a hoarse cry, turned her head toward the object and began licking away the glossy covering. Ryan watched in amazement as the bundle moved and raised its small head. It was a baby seal, a pup.

The pup lay there for a moment, its head turning from side to side in bewilderment. Then, guided by instinct, it moved awkwardly on its flippers to the shadowy bulk of its mother. The pup pushed and nuzzled its snout into its mother's side, and milk began trickling from the corners of its mouth.

The mother seal spread out in a comfortable position, laid her head down, and dozed. Ryan smiled as a snore like an old man's sounded from the animal.

Ryan watched the mother and her baby for a long time. The sun was low in the sky when he retraced his steps around the point and climbed the bank to the cliff opening leading toward home. He had a warm feeling inside as he thought of the birth he had just witnessed.

He wanted to share the seals with Cilla, but she wouldn't be able to resist telling others. The mother seal and her pup needed privacy. There was only one person he could trust.

The following Saturday morning, after his father had gone to the office "just to catch up," Ryan worked with his mother in the family's overgrown garden. Still angry from an exchange of words with Ryan's father, she slammed a spade into the compacted ground, loosening the soil around clumps of weeds, then grasped them at their base and ripped them out. Ryan and his mother worked together in silence, with only an occasional grunt as one of them did battle with a particularly stubborn weed.

Now and then, Ryan glanced at his mother, noticing the tight line of her lips soften as the physical effort and the smell of freshly turned soil eased her tension. After a time, she straightened and wiped the back of her hand across her forehead, streaking her skin with mud.

"Why don't we go for a swim?" Ryan asked.

"Now that's a very good idea," she said, smiling at him.

"I'll take you somewhere special," he said.

They made their way over the headland. "This way," said Ryan, scrambling up the boulder next to the cliff face.

"I didn't know this was here," his mother said as they wriggled through the tunnel.

They slid down the far side of the cliff and were picking their way over rocks, toward the point, when Ryan touched his mother's arm.

"Follow me quietly, Mom," he said. "I want to show you something."

They rounded the point and Ryan scanned the bay. Nothing disturbed the curve of secluded sand. Disappointment rose in his throat.

Then he saw them. The mother seal lay nestled among low rocks on the far side of the bay, suckling her pup.

"Look," he said, pointing toward the seals. "Over there."

"They're beautiful," she exclaimed.

They watched the seals in silence. Sun slanted across the rocks, and the mother seal stretched out to absorb its warmth.

"What a rich chestnut coat the mother has," Ryan's mother said. "It shines like copper."

"Copper," said Ryan. "That can be her name."

"It's unusual for a seal to give birth away from a rookery," his mother observed. "She must have gone into labor on her way to join other seals."

Ryan and his mother moved onto the sandy bay. The mother seal raised herself on her flippers, tossed her head, and snorted a warning. The pup fixed huge, solemn eyes on the intruders as though it was assessing them.

"Let's go for our swim," said Ryan's mother. "Maybe Copper will think we're just another seal and her pup."

"I'm a teenager," Ryan protested. "You can't call me a pup."

They tossed their T-shirts on the sand and ran to the ocean. The shallow waters of the bay were warm, but as they swam out to the breakers, the cold ocean currents swirled in and made them gasp. They dived into the rolling surf and came up shivering and laughing.

"Wow, it's cold," gasped Ryan.

They swam and splashed around until Ryan's teeth chattered and his legs felt numb. "I'm getting out now," he called.

They lay on the sand, warming themselves in the sun. "I used to swim a lot with your father," his mother said, "before he got too busy at work to spare the time." She sighed. "He often said I swam like a seal. He called me his selkie."

"What's a selkie?"

"It's an old Celtic name for a seal," she said. "The Celts have an ancient legend about selkies."

"Do you know the legend?"

"Your father's mother told your dad the selkie story when he was a boy." She looked at Ryan. "Ask him about it sometime." His mother's dark eyes seemed deep and pensive, like the seal pup's, like a selkie, thought Ryan.

"That's what I'll call the pup," he said, "Selkie."

"Copper and Selkie," his mother said. "That's a good choice."

They gathered their things and left the beach under the watchful gaze of the seals.

When school had let out for the summer break, Cilla had gone away with her family. Ryan missed her bossy good nature. It was strange not to have her bursting in the door and shouting, "Surf's up, get your wet suit and board," or, "Come on, let's go fishing." He found himself thinking about his friend a lot and was surprised at how much he missed her.

During the summer, Ryan had visited the seals often. At first, Copper was wary. Ryan would go for a swim, then return and stretch out on the sand at a respectful distance. Within days, Copper had accepted his presence and ignored him as he gradually moved closer.

Ryan often watched as Selkie explored the rock pools in the bay. The pup would dip its face in a pool, shake its head, and bleat in surprise. Once, it leaned over too far and fell into a pool. It splashed and struggled for a few moments, then it rolled and began to play in the shallow water as it discovered its natural element.

Now, as Ryan emerged from the access tunnel, he remembered the hurt on Cilla's face when he wouldn't let her come with him today. He longed to share the seals with her, but his mother had warned him not to tell anyone else. "Copper and Selkie need to be protected," she had said. "The more people who know the seals are here, the more at risk they'll be."

At least it would be peaceful at the bay, and he could practice his harmonica. Ryan rounded the point and stopped. A small fishing boat lay drawn up on the sand.

Chapter 2

Across the bay, Ryan saw a man walking slowly toward the rocks on which Copper and Selkie usually basked in the sun. Today, they were nowhere in sight.

Ryan jumped onto the sand and began running toward the man, anxious to stop him before he discovered any trace of the seals.

"Hi there," he called.

The man turned around. "Where did you come from?" His face wrinkled in surprise.

Ryan avoided the question. "The fishing's not much good around here," he said.

"I know," the man said. "But I'm curious about a seal and its pup that I saw on the rocks when I went past late yesterday. The sea was too high to come in for a look."

"You must have mistaken one of these rocks for a seal."

"There's no mistaking a seal up on its flippers." The man rubbed his bristly chin. "And the pup was a little one, slight, with a small head. It just might be a female, too." He looked at Ryan. "What brings you here?"

"I like a bit of peace and quiet."

The man nodded as if he understood completely. "Ben Kelly's the name." He stuck out a hand. "What's yours?"

"Ryan." He shook Kelly's hand, surprised by the hard grip of the older man.

Kelly looked over at the rocks. "You haven't seen any seals, have you?"

"I've seen some of the stuffed ones in the maritime museum."

"Lovely coats, seals have," Kelly said. "Nearly was their downfall."

"What do you mean?"

"Sealers slaughtered them by the thousands last century." Kelly drew a tobacco pouch and papers from his pocket. He flicked out a paper and spread stringy tobacco along its middle. "The rocks ran red with their blood."

"Why? Why did they kill them?" asked Ryan.

"People liked to wrap themselves up in warm, cozy seal furs." Kelly rolled the paper into a thin tube and licked the gummed edge, then continued.

"And people filled their lamps with the oil from sea elephants." He took a box of matches from his pocket. "A lot of money was made from seals in those days, but a man had to search long and hard for them when I was young." He struck a match, cupped his hands around the flame to guard it from the breeze, and guided it to the cigarette in his mouth.

Ryan noticed the man's leather boots with soft fur tops. "Isn't it against the law to kill seals?"

"The last open season was years ago, and apart from a bit of poaching, the seals have been left to breed like rabbits," Kelly said. "But that might all change soon."

"Why should it? What possible harm does a seal do to anyone?"

"It takes a lot of fish to fill a seal's belly. They put a fisherman's livelihood at risk." Kelly drew on his cigarette. "There's talk of a culling season to get their numbers down."

Ryan shuddered. Culling season or killing season, it meant the same thing – slaughter. Ryan avoided glancing at the rocks. Where were the seals? he asked himself. He turned his back on Kelly. "I'm going for a swim."

"A word of warning," said Kelly. "The mother seal must be away feeding, but when she returns, don't get between her and the sea. A seal will charge anything that blocks its escape route."

A movement on the shoreline caught Ryan's eye. "Look! Your boat's starting to drift."

"Blast!" muttered Kelly as he hurried over the sand. He pulled his boat into the surf and leaped in. The motor sprang to life, and he headed out beyond the waves.

Ryan stood on the beach until the boat was out of sight. Then he raced over the rocks, calling, "Copper, Selkie. Where are you?"

As he searched, he tried to imitate the sound he had heard Selkie make when calling to Copper, a warbling *ba-aa,* like a lamb. He explored the entire area, calling, but without response.

If Ben Kelly had seen the seals and found his way into the bay, who else might have been here? Troubled, Ryan sat in the shade of the bushes growing at the foot of the bluff that sheltered the sweep of the bay. He took out his harmonica. Music usually helped to clear his thoughts.

Ryan played a few bars, and the notes rang across the bay. He ran his mouth up and down the instrument, blowing hard to clear any obstruction, then played the opening chords of a blues tune. An off-key tremor rose above his music. He lowered the harmonica and listened.

At first Ryan thought the squawking sound was from a seagull. Then it seemed to sharpen into a cry. Selkie! It had to be Selkie, Ryan thought. He looked around, but there was no movement.

A wail sounded behind him, and he felt the hairs on his neck rise. He turned to face the bluff, which formed a solid wall. He parted the bushes, the spiky branches scratching his arms. At the base of the steep bank, a small cave opening stretched back into darkness.

Ryan bent over and squeezed through the narrow entrance. Inside, the cave opened out into a dome-shaped grotto. After his eyes adjusted to the darkness, he saw a shape against the far wall.

Selkie lay in a dejected huddle. Ryan moved toward the pup, making soothing noises. She raised her head and bleated.

"Take it easy; you're safe now," he whispered and stroked her head. "You've been exploring, haven't you?" After a moment, the pup laid her snout on his sneakers.

Ryan sat comforting Selkie for a few minutes, then he gently nudged her toward the mouth of the cave. She balked at going through the opening, so Ryan went out first and turned to encourage the pup. He could see her snout wrinkling at the smell of fresh air and her whiskers sizing the gap for body width.

Slowly, she emerged into the daylight. The pup's small ears drooped, and tears trickled from the corners of her eyes. She shook herself, snuffled, and headed for the rocks. She scuttled forward, using her front flippers in an awkward windmill motion. Waves splashed over the rocks, filling the pools with each swish of the incoming tide.

The pup slid into a pool, reveling in the soothing water. Ryan sat on the edge of the pool, careful not to frighten her. She gazed at him with coal black eyes. He eased himself into the pool and lowered his face into the water, level with Selkie's black button nose.

As they stared at one another, Ryan sensed a communication between them. Selkie flicked a flipper, splashing him. He imitated the pup by slapping his hand on the surface. Together, they splashed and played in the sun-warmed pool.

A shrill, penetrating cry sounded across the bay. Ryan looked up to see Copper at the water's edge. She stood raised up on her front flippers, snout pointing to the sky. Her wet coat shone, and her plump sides showed the success of her feeding trip. Again her sharp call rang out.

Selkie gave a *ba-aa* in response and struggled out of the water. Copper shook herself and made her way up the beach. Ryan was surprised at the speed of her approach. She moved quickly on all fours, with her back flippers turned forward. He hauled himself from the pool, anxious to put distance between himself and the mother seal. In his hurry to escape, he slipped on the rocks and scraped his shin and his hand. Then he scrambled to his feet and ran.

From the safety of the point, he looked back. Selkie was burrowing into Copper's side, guzzling her rich milk.

That night, Ryan's mother received a call from a friend who lived near her mother's remote seaside home. She listened intently for a while, a frown creasing her lips. When she replaced the receiver, she turned to her husband, her face serious.

"Mother is very ill," she said. "She needs me at home with her."

"Of course," Ryan's father said. "Ryan and I can manage for a few days."

"I might very well be away longer than that," she answered.

"Oh?" Ryan's father sounded wary. He turned his face away from his wife.

Ryan's mother kept her head down for a moment, then looked at her husband for a long time. Finally, she spoke, "Time apart will be good for us both."

"Take all the time you need," his father said, and Ryan heard the pain in his voice. "Maybe you'll feel happier when you come back."

"I might not want to come back," his mother said very softly.

Ryan's father turned away quickly, his mouth a hard line. He strode from the room, slamming the door behind him. Anxiety knotted in Ryan's chest. He hurried to his room, turned on his stereo, and took out his harmonica. His feet tapped out a rhythm as he began to play, and the music flowed through him, soothing him and blotting out the turmoil in his mind.

In the morning, when his mother hugged Ryan good-bye, he held her tight, wondering when he would see her again. "Look after Copper and Selkie," she said. She reached up and patted his cheek. "And take care of yourself."

The school day passed in a haze, one subject blurring into another. His English teacher noticed his blank page at creative writing time. "Writer's block?" he said. "You can work on it at home tonight and hand it in tomorrow."

After school, Cilla caught up with him. "Do you want company on the way home?"

"If you can keep up," he said, relieved that she wasn't still annoyed with him.

She poked out her tongue and cycled along the road beside him. They stopped at an intersection leading to the coast. "You're quiet," she said.

"My grandmother's ill," Ryan said. "Mom's gone to look after her for a while."

Cilla noticed his strained face and made no further comment. The houses thinned out as they passed through the outskirts of town. They turned onto a side road heading toward the coast. The air became heavy with salt spray. Ryan licked his lips and tasted the sharp tang. They kept going until the road veered past a sign that read, "Ocean Vista – No Exit."

Several wooden houses stood among the dunes overlooking a stretch of sand leading to the ocean. They bicycled past houses to the end of the road and stopped outside a small cottage. A pathway edged with flowers led to an open door that was painted bright yellow. The house looked very friendly and welcoming.

"It looks like your mother's at home," Ryan said.

"Briefly," Cilla said, making a face. "She's the doctor on duty for the late shift at the hospital, so

I get to look after my baby brother until Dad comes home."

"Lucky you," said Ryan, laughing at Cilla's scowl. "See you tomorrow."

Ryan walked his bicycle across the road to his house, which stood apart, isolated and shaded by trees. He tugged at a loose board by the back door and took out a key.

The quiet house overwhelmed him. He had an urge to yell and shout, to fill the silent shell with sound. Instead, he flopped onto the couch and turned on the television. Cartoon characters flickered across the screen in a hypnotic whirl of color. He let his eyes close.

It was dark outside when he awoke to the sound of a car door slamming and footsteps on the porch.

"Sorry I'm late." His father set a paper bag on the table. "I stopped off to get fish and chips."

Ryan noticed the gray streaking his dad's flame red hair as his father bent over the bag of food.

"Come on, Ryan. Dive in before it gets cold."

Ryan pulled out a chair and sat down. He swallowed a chunk of lukewarm fish and felt it settle in the pit of his stomach.

"I'll make you some coffee," he said as his father's head drooped sleepily over the mound of congealing food.

Chapter 3

The following evening, Ryan's father came home early with a bundle of papers. He stacked them on the kitchen table and sat hunched over them, making notes and calculations.

Ryan inspected the fridge and found a packet of bacon and some eggs.

"I'll cook," he said. His father grunted in reply. Great response, Dad, thought Ryan. He wondered how often his mother had been hurt by the same casual indifference.

Ryan served the meal and sat down opposite his father, who pushed his papers aside and picked up his knife and fork. "This looks good," he said, and gave a smile of approval.

Ryan remembered the pleasure he had known as a child when his father would come home from work and greet him with a smile. Those had been good days. The house had been filled with laughter, and his parents would sit talking for hours in the evening. Sometimes they would all go outside and wait for the first star to appear. "Make a wish," his mother would say when they saw it.

Ryan brewed coffee and waited until his father relaxed back in his chair with the mug cupped in his hands. "Dad, Mom said to ask you about the selkie story that Nana Campbell used to tell you."

His father raised his eyebrows. "I'm surprised your mother remembers the selkies." He drew in a deep breath, then gazed out the window at the night sky and began to speak in a faraway voice.

"It is said that one day a year, the seals leave the ocean, shed their skins, and take human form. The selkies, as they're known, then play and sing and dance along the rocky shore.

"One such day, a lonely fisherman chanced upon the selkies and fell in love with the most beautiful of them all, a young woman with soft brown eyes and long, flowing hair. He stole her discarded sealskin and hid it in a cave.

"The fisherman crouched behind the rocks and waited. At sundown, he watched the selkies slip into their sealskins one by one and slide into the ocean – all except one, the woman with whom he had fallen in love. As she searched the shore for her skin, he stepped out from hiding. 'Come live with me,' he said. 'Be my wife and I will take good care of you.'

"Unable to return to the sea without her sealskin, the selkie woman agreed to become the fisherman's wife. Many seasons passed, and she gave birth to a son. He grew into a fine boy, with soft dark eyes and golden brown skin. The woman loved her son very much but yearned to return to her own kind."

Ryan's father lowered his head and gazed into his empty cup for a long time. He was silent for so long, that Ryan wondered if he had forgotten the story. Then his father sighed and continued.

"One night the boy dreamed he heard a voice calling him. 'Come down to the ocean, my boy. Come down to the sea.' The boy got up and made his way to a rocky headland. Just before dawn an old seal rose from the waves and spoke to him. 'Look over in the cave, my boy. Take what is there and give it to your mother.'

"Rays from the rising sun shone into a nearby cave. The boy found a bundle tied with fishing line hidden inside. He unwrapped it and out rolled a silky, golden brown sealskin. Clutching it to him, he returned home.

"When the lad arrived home his father had already left on a fishing trip. At the sight of her sealskin, his mother wept.

"'Come with me, my selkie son,' she said. They hurried to the shore, where she slipped into the skin and, turning his face toward hers, breathed long and deep into his lungs. Then, taking his hand, she drew him into the ocean with her.

"Deeper and deeper they descended. At first, the boy was alarmed, but he soon found he could breathe beneath the ocean. They passed many wonderful underwater sights, until at last, they began to swim upward and finally surfaced in a huge cavern.

"There on a tall rock sat the old seal who had called to him. 'This is my father, your grandfather,' his mother said.

"After several happy days in the seal kingdom, the boy's mother drew him to her. 'You are of human flesh, my selkie son. You must return to the land. But go to the rocks on nights of the full moon. Call to me and I will come.' She wept as they parted. 'Go now with love in your heart for your father, for he was very kind to me in our many years together.'"

Ryan's father rubbed his forehead in a weary gesture. Outside, Ryan heard the cry of a lone seabird. His father cleared his throat, then carried on in a tired voice. "The boy's father grieved over the loss of his beloved wife for the rest of his days. The selkie boy grew into a handsome young fisherman with soft, flowing hair and warm brown eyes. Whenever he went fishing, his nets were always filled. And on nights of the full moon, he can still be heard calling from the rocky headland. By and by, a seal will rise from the ocean and talk with him."

They sat in silence for a while, each lost in his own thoughts, until Ryan's father pushed back his chair.

"Time for bed," he said, then went into his room, closing the door behind him.

A storm lashed the coast in the following days. In the mornings, Ryan and Cilla were blown to school on their bicycles, and in the afternoons, they struggled home against gale-force winds. High tides lapped the sand dunes sheltering Ocean Vista and cut off access to the headland. Marine broadcasts warned all craft against going to sea. At least Copper and Selkie will be safe in the bay, thought Ryan.

At first, after all the arguments, it had been almost a relief to live in a silent house. But as the days rolled by, a cloud of dejection settled over Ryan. His father became quieter and more withdrawn. He came home late in the evenings with a pile of paperwork.

Ryan wished he could see his mother and talk with her again. His grandmother refused to have a telephone. "I've got plenty of time to write letters to people with whom I want to keep in touch," she always said.

Twice his mother had walked to a neighbor's place to phone him after he had come home from school. She sounded distant, and their conversation was awkward. After each call, he hung up feeling even more alone.

As the storm dragged on, Ryan paced the house with restless energy. He directed his attention to the dirty kitchen. His mother would hate to see the mess that had built up in her absence. He turned the hot water on full, added detergent, and swept dishes into the sink with a clatter.

He had washed a pile of dishes and was starting to scrub the stove when someone knocked on the door. Without waiting for him to reply, Cilla pushed the door open and entered the kitchen. Ryan tossed her a towel.

"You're just in time to help," he said.

"You're not my boss," she protested. "Mom's off duty, so I came over here to escape my baby brother."

"At least you've got a family," said Ryan.

"Have you heard when your mother's coming back?" Cilla began to dry some of the dishes.

Ryan shook his head. He hadn't told Cilla he wasn't sure his mother would ever come home. If he said it out loud, it would make it seem real, maybe final. He made cocoa for them both, and they stretched out on the carpet in the living room, listening to music. Ryan sipped his cocoa, enjoying the nearness of his friend and the warmth she brought into the house.

The storm eased the next day. When Cilla and Ryan cycled home after school, the ocean had calmed considerably.

"Great surf," Cilla said. "Let's go surfing."

Ryan hesitated. He had hoped to visit the bay to see how the seals had weathered the storm.

Cilla turned her head away from him. "Well, if you don't want to..." She sounded hurt.

"Of course I do," Ryan said hastily. "I'll meet you on the beach in five minutes."

When he pushed open the back door, the house smelled musty and damp. He flung his backpack on the table, grabbed a piece of bread to eat, and pulled on his wet suit.

The phone rang, loud and insistent. It was probably his mother. He went to answer it, then changed his mind. Perhaps she would worry about him if he didn't answer. Maybe she would even come home.

Fat chance, he thought. He slammed the door on the jangling of the phone. Taking his board, he raced down the beach and headed into the surf with Cilla. The waves met them head-on. Ryan let them wash over him in a blast of ice-cold clarity. He paddled out to the swelling breakers, turned, then caught a curling, plummeting wave that tossed him onto the shore. Time after time, they challenged the waves.

One powerful wave dumped Cilla into the shallows, rolling her over and throwing her board onto the beach. She scrambled to her feet, water flowing from her glistening wet suit. Her hair clung to her face and rivulets of water trickled down her neck. She's like a selkie, thought Ryan, watching as Cilla pushed her hair back and smiled at him. She retrieved her board and raced back into the ocean.

The wispy clouds were streaked with red from the setting sun when they finally made their way up the beach.

"See you tomorrow," Ryan called to Cilla as he trudged away through the sand dunes. He dumped his board on the porch and peeled off his wet suit, ready for a shower.

He had just stepped out of the shower when he heard his father call, "Ryan! Where are you?"

"I'm right here, Dad," he answered. He came out, pulling on his jeans. "You're home pretty early for a change."

"I've bought steak and fries for dinner."

At least we'll eat well, thought Ryan. The phone rang again.

"You get it, Dad," he said. "I'll cook."

His father answered the phone. His drooping shoulders lifted as he listened for a moment. Then he said, "Yes, Ryan's here. We're managing all right." There was another pause before he said, "Okay, I'll tell him." He replaced the receiver and turned to Ryan. "Your mother sends you her love."

Ryan flipped the steaks in the pan. "How's Grandma doing?"

"Pretty much the same it seems."

No chance of Mom coming home soon then, thought Ryan.

Chapter 4

On Wednesday morning, Ryan surfaced from a dream in which he was swimming underwater with a shadowy seal shape gliding alongside him. A sound had woke him, a voice. He thought he had heard his name spoken. He lay floating in a half-asleep, half-awake state, still cradled in the silky smooth ocean. He heard the voice again.

It was his father making a phone call. "I'll see you soon. Bye."

At breakfast, his father said, "I'm going away tomorrow on business." He paused, sounding unsure. "At this stage it's just an overnight trip, and I should be back Friday evening. But other matters could keep me away over the weekend. I may not be home until Monday evening."

"That's okay with me."

"I'll ask Cilla Hansen's mother if you can stay at their house."

The idea of staying at Cilla's appealed to Ryan, but then he remembered Copper and Selkie. If he stayed at Cilla's, he would never be able to escape to the bay by himself.

"That could be a problem for them," he said. "They haven't got a spare room, so I would be sleeping in the baby's room, and he cries a lot. Besides, Mr. and Mrs. Hansen have enough to do looking after the baby without me underfoot."

"I'm not happy about leaving you on your own."

"Dad, you work late most nights and leave me at home by myself," Ryan protested.

"True, but you can always phone me at work if you run into any kind of a problem," his father said defensively.

"How about if I promise to phone the Hansens if I need anything while you're away?"

"That sounds fine for overnight," his father conceded. "But I could be away all weekend."

"I can take care of myself for a few days," said Ryan. "I'm not a kid, Dad."

"I don't suppose you are." Ryan's father looked thoughtfully at his teenage son. "You do seem to have grown up in the past few months."

"Then let me prove I can manage by myself while you're away," said Ryan. "After all, the Hansens are just across the road if I need them."

"I'll give Cilla's mother a call this evening and see what can be arranged," his father said. "I guess you can't get into too much trouble in a quiet backwater like Ocean Vista."

"Thanks, Dad," said Ryan. "And you don't need to worry about me getting up for school on Monday if you're not home. Next week is a school holiday, so I'll just be hanging around here anyway."

Ryan's father stood up and picked up his briefcase. "I'll see you this evening."

When Ryan got home from school, he paused at the kitchen door and studied the quiet room. The house felt empty and lifeless. Throwing his backpack on the floor, he sank into a kitchen chair. He couldn't call this place a home anymore. It just seemed like a cage in which he ate and slept. Ryan's anger flared, and he slammed his hands against the table. Flinging back his chair, he went to the sink and splashed cold water on his face. He gasped and shook his head.

Outside, beyond the sand dunes, the ocean crashed onto the beach. Copper and Selkie came to

Ryan's mind. He wanted to make sure they were all right. He remembered how Ben Kelly had said that seals were a threat to fishermen.

Ryan went outside and dragged his father's dinghy from the shed. He put in a can of gas, his fishing gear, and some bait, then hauled the boat down to the beach. His father had taught him how to handle the boat in rough seas, but he had also cautioned Ryan frequently against taking the dinghy out alone.

But Ryan didn't feel up to the long walk over the headland and through the tunnel to the bay. Provided that all went well, he would be back before his father came home, and if he was lucky enough to catch a fish for dinner, perhaps that would appease his father.

Ryan put on a life jacket and pushed the dinghy into the surf. He jumped into the boat and pulled the outboard's starter cord. The motor coughed and died. Ryan tugged on the cord again and this time the engine sprang to life.

He turned the boat away from Ocean Vista and steered a course wide of the headland and submerged rocks. Waves crossed the bow, and spray cascaded over him.

As the dinghy putted past the sheer cliff, Ryan looked across the water at the boulder masking the hidden tunnel. The cliff face looked impenetrable from the sea. On the far side of the cliff, small trees and bushes screened the tunnel exit leading down to the rocky shoreline.

Ahead lay the point, and beyond that, the bay. Ryan nosed the boat toward the point, and his spirits lifted at the thought of seeing Copper and Selkie again. He skirted the rocks, and the bay opened out in front of him. Sheltered by the bluff behind and edged by rocks on both sides, the slender curve of sand looked deserted.

He rode the dinghy into the shallows, cut the motor, and jumped over the side. He dragged the boat onto the beach and looked around.

Copper lay on a rock, sunbathing. The pup stretched back over her mother, her stomach exposed and front flippers flopped to either side. Selkie's glossy underbelly glinted in the sun. She lay at peace, her face raised to the sun's warmth. Ryan chuckled as the pup fanned herself with her flippers, which looked ridiculously like wings.

Copper stirred and Ryan drew back. The mother seal humped and bumped until Selkie wriggled away from her. Then she raised herself on her front flippers and waddled over the rocks, toward the ocean.

Selkie followed, bleating and yelping. It amazed Ryan how quickly the pup had grown in her few months of life. She now had a firm, compact body with a finely shaped head and inquisitive face. Her jet black birth coat had molted and lightened to a silvery gray.

Copper paused and lifted her rear flipper to scratch vigorously behind her neck. Selkie reached her side, and Copper nudged her pup toward the waves surging against the rocks. Selkie whined and raised her soulful eyes in protest. Copper slid into the churning ocean, turned, and swung her head in a beckoning gesture.

The pup drew her body weight back onto her rear flippers, refusing to enter the rough sea. Copper barked sharply and Selkie edged forward. Further and further she leaned, dipping her head into the slapping waves until at last she tumbled in. She struggled for a moment, then her sleek body disappeared under the surface.

Seconds later Selkie's dark, torpedo-shaped head resurfaced. Rolling and gliding, she frolicked in the ocean. She skimmed through the water, using her rear flippers to change direction.

Ryan watched her plunge into a dive, her hind flippers flicking above the foam like small flags. It surprised him how quickly a creature so awkward on land could transform into a graceful mermaid. No wonder the selkie woman in his father's story had longed to return to her ocean home.

A rough wave thrust Selkie against the rocks and she decided she'd had enough. She clambered out and shook herself, spinning out a halo of spray, then flapped over to a warm rock.

Ryan suddenly realized that shadows from the bluff had begun to spread over the bay. He needed to leave now if he wanted to return home before his father. He turned around and heard something crunch beneath his feet.

A matchbox lay crushed on the hard sand. Ryan frowned. He remembered Ben Kelly using a similar box of matches. Kelly must have come back, but he hadn't harmed the seals. Copper could have been away fishing, and perhaps Selkie had taken shelter in the cave again.

Ryan pushed the dinghy into the surf, jumped on board, and started the motor. He steered into the deep water out past the point. Opposite the cliff, he cut the engine, baited a hook, and lowered his line overboard.

Within a few minutes, Ryan felt a sharp tug and his line went tight. He hauled in his catch, a fat blue cod. He whacked the struggling fish on the head and laid it in the bottom of the boat.

Dark clouds began to gather as he pulled on the starter cord. The engine turned over once, hesitated, sputtered, and died. He pulled the cord again. The motor gave a half-hearted chug and stopped.

"Oh no," Ryan muttered. "Now I've flooded the engine."

The dinghy began to drift. Ryan scrabbled in the bottom of the boat, found the two oars, and fit them in the oarlocks. Sculling with one oar, he turned the stern toward the headland. Then he bent forward and pulled back on both oars.

He made slow progress against the strong current and choppy sea. When the heavy clouds let down a splatter of rain, he was soon soaked. His wet T-shirt rubbed under his arms as he rowed.

Dusk had fallen by the time Ryan sighted lights along the shore. The outline of his house stood in darkness. Relieved, he strained on the oars until he was over the swell of the surf. He hauled the dinghy up the beach and through a small gap in the sand dunes.

Car lights swept into the drive as he stowed the boat in the shed. Fish in hand, he reached the porch at the same time as his father.

"Ryan!" His father's face was stern. "Have you been out in the dinghy by yourself?"

"I thought you would like fresh fish tonight."

His father opened the door and switched on the kitchen light. "I appreciate that, Ryan, but it's dangerous to go out alone, especially after dark," he said. "Please don't go out alone in the boat again while I'm gone."

"Okay, Dad," Ryan held up his hand. "Okay."

Later, as he washed the dishes and his father dried, Ryan wondered if it would always be just the two of them, like Copper and Selkie. His parents seemed so different from each other, maybe they would never be happy living together again.

"Dad, how did you and Mom meet?"

"I was on vacation on the coast when I first saw her. She was up to her neck in the ocean, holding on to one end of a flounder net." He paused in the midst of drying a pot. "I thought she was the most beautiful woman I had ever seen, so I swam out to talk to her." He grinned. "The guy on the other end of the net got really mad and roared at me to get out of the way. Then I got tangled in the net, and she ended up hauling me to shore."

"You made a lousy first impression," laughed Ryan. "How did you get over that?"

"She said later I was the biggest fish she had ever caught and she just couldn't bear to throw me back." His father smiled wryly. "I pestered her until she agreed to marry me, and we came back here. It was our own slice of paradise, hidden from the rest of the world. We were really happy..." His voice trailed off.

"What happened?"

His father shrugged. "Business has been bad the last year or so. I've had to spend more time at work and take trips away from home," he said. "I guess your mother got lonely and homesick."

"Maybe it's like the selkie story," said Ryan. "She needed to go back to her own place for a while."

But what if she doesn't come back, he thought. Where would I fit in? I'm her son. Would she leave me here or take me with her? But then I would have to leave Dad – and Cilla.

Ryan sighed. It was too messy, too hard for him to figure out. Anyway, he would have to go along with whatever his parents decided, until he was old enough to take charge of his own life. He put away the dishes while his father phoned Cilla's mother.

Ryan caught parts of the conversation, then heard his father say, "Well, that's great. Thanks a lot." His father replaced the receiver and turned to Ryan. "Mrs. Hansen will be at home over the weekend. She's happy to keep an eye on you and help out if you need anything. She's on call this Sunday, but she says that's usually a quiet day, so she should be around most of the time."

"That's great," said Ryan.

"I'm trusting you to act responsibly, Ryan," his father said. "Don't let me down."

"I won't, Dad."

Bicycling to school with Cilla on Thursday morning, Ryan recalled his father's farewell. His dad had been edgy. Although he often went on business trips, something was different this time. Ryan remembered his father's phone call the previous morning and how he thought he had heard his name spoken. Ryan wondered if there was a connection.

"Your father called yesterday," Cilla said, as if she was reading his mind. "He said he was going away and asked Mom and Dad if they would mind helping if you need anything."

"He seems to think I'll have trouble managing on my own," Ryan said.

"At least he made sure someone is looking out for you."

"I suppose so," said Ryan.

Ryan's attention strayed during his morning classes. He thought about his father saying business had been bad. Maybe that was why his dad had been so uptight when he left. It must be pretty rough to see both your marriage and your work fall apart, Ryan thought.

At lunch he headed for the school pool. As he swam, the shadow of his body shimmered along the bottom of the pool. He remembered the shadowy form swimming alongside him in his dream, and he wondered what it would be like to glide through the ocean with Selkie.

Later, Ryan searched for marine mammals in the school library's computer subject index. A search for books about the underwater world and its creatures revealed two books on seals. He checked them out at the front desk.

After the last bell, Cilla joined him on the sidewalk leading to the bicycle rack.

"Dad gave me some money for extra food and stuff," Ryan said. "Do you want to come shopping with me?"

Cilla shook her head. "I have to look after my baby brother again. I think I should change my name to Cinderella."

At the supermarket, Ryan scanned the shelves for a few easy-to-prepare foods. He paid at the checkout, filled his backpack, and bicycled home.

That evening, he lay on the floor in the living room with the books he had borrowed from the library. Legends and folklore surrounded seals. Some cultures believed seals were capable of understanding the voice of the ocean waves, and considered them to be the link between sea creatures and humans. Ryan read about seals' intelligence and keen sense of hearing.

He hadn't realized there were so many kinds of seals, all with different habits. Some breeds fed their pups for a few weeks before leaving them to fend for themselves, whereas fur seal pups continued to suckle their mothers' rich, oily milk for months. Although human greed had nearly caused the extinction of fur seals, the pups were also hunted by one of their own kind – spotted leopard seals. It reminded Ryan of the white mice he once had that ate their own young. Even parents couldn't always be trusted, he thought.

The phone rang on Friday morning as Ryan was preparing for school.

"Hello, Ryan. Everything all right?" His father's voice sounded distant.

"No problems," Ryan reassured him.

"Good. That's good." His father seemed preoccupied. "I'm sorry, Ryan, but I will need to stay away for the weekend. Will you be okay until I come home on Monday night?"

"Sure, Dad."

"Call the Hansens and let them know, all right? Look after yourself. Bye."

Ryan hung up, feeling alienated. He shrugged. So what if my father is immersed in his own world, Ryan thought. It leaves me free to do whatever I want for the weekend.

Cilla was unusually quiet as they bicycled home together after school.

"What's wrong?" Ryan asked.

"I'm going to fail history," she replied. "I'm hopeless at remembering dates."

"Come over when you're finished baby-sitting," Ryan suggested. "We can study together."

"Great. It'll be much quieter at your place," she said and waved as she turned into her driveway. "See you later."

Ryan arrived at his house, whistling. He let himself into the silent house. Late afternoon sun shone through the crystal his mother had hung in front of the kitchen window. Rainbow colors whirled around the room. He cleared away his breakfast dishes and started to make dinner. His weekend was off to a good start.

Chapter 5

*R*yan felt a bite in the autumn wind as he clambered up the headland on Saturday morning. He looked over his shoulder, checking for Cilla. Apart from a dog roaming around the sand dunes, the beach appeared to be deserted.

Hoisting his backpack further up his shoulders, Ryan continued over the rocks to the sandy inlet overshadowed by the cliff. The access tunnel offered shelter from the wind, but when he emerged on the other side, a sharp gust made him shiver. He slid down the bank and picked his way around the point, to the bay.

He smiled when he saw Copper and Selkie playing in the ocean. Copper was floating on her back in a quiet eddy while Selkie nosed up out of the water and launched herself onto her mother. Copper wrapped her flippers around her pup, clasping Selkie to her chest. For several seconds, they drifted together, then Copper rolled over and Selkie tumbled into the water.

Ryan moved toward the seals, eased off his pack, and took out his father's camera. Keeping a cautious distance, he photographed the pair at play. They spiraled, twisted, and dived so swiftly, he was unsure whether he had captured their graceful, fluid movements.

Tiring of the game, Copper headed toward the shore and hauled herself out of the ocean. Snout skyward, she gave the strangled bark that Ryan first heard several months ago, shook herself, and hitched over to the rocks. Selkie flapped after her, yapping. Copper turned to snap at her pup.

Ryan was startled by a dark streak that flashed past and launched itself at Selkie. He recognized the dog he had seen earlier on the sand dunes. It must have picked up his scent and followed him through the tunnel.

The dog sunk its fangs deep into the seal pup's neck. Selkie yelped and whined, shaking her body in an attempt to free herself.

Copper roared and darted her head toward the dog. It edged away, still clinging to Selkie. Copper lunged forward, swinging her head from side to side, and slashed the dog on its shoulder. It howled and released Selkie, who let out a *ba-aa* and scurried behind her mother, blood trickling down her neck.

Incensed, the dog turned and sprang at Copper's throat. Ryan picked up a hunk of driftwood and ran toward them.

"Get away, you mongrel!" he shouted, whacking the dog's back. Its grip loosened and Copper shook herself free.

Barking insanely, the dog continued to torment Copper, looking for a way to dart behind her and attack Selkie. The dog ran back and forth, changing direction swiftly and staying just out of Copper's reach. Then Selkie cried out and Copper turned her head.

In that instant, the dog hurled itself at Copper, clinging to her neck, and biting into the flesh around her ear. Blood spurted from the wound, and the seal bellowed. Selkie scuttled for the shelter of the bluff.

Copper reared up, swinging her body. The dog began to slip and clawed at the seal's head, gouging her right eye. In agony, she swayed wildly. The dog slid to the ground in front of her. Copper's head came down, and she clamped her jaws around the dog's leg. She shook it, and Ryan heard a snap.

As the dog hobbled away, Copper lumbered after it. She moved in an uneven gait, hampered by the lack of sight in her injured eye.

Powerless to help Copper, Ryan grabbed his pack and made for the bluff, in search of Selkie. As he approached the entrance to the cave, he heard the sound of a motor. He turned and scanned the bay, spotting Kelly's boat as it came around the point, waves slapping its sides. Ducking into the cave, Ryan found Selkie huddled against the wall. The pup whimpered as he came near. In the dim light, her eyes were huge dark globes.

Ryan heard the boat chug closer to the shore. He guessed Kelly must have seen Copper by now.

The boat's motor shut off and a roar from Copper sounded a warning to the newcomer. Selkie trembled and whined.

"Quiet now," Ryan whispered. "We can't let Kelly know we're here." He cradled the pup and stroked her head, avoiding the patch of blood on her neck where the dog had bitten her. Selkie's eyes began to close and her head drooped.

Kelly won't dare go near Copper while she's enraged from her injuries, Ryan thought. He eased the sleeping seal to the cave floor and moved to the entrance. Crouching low, he peered through the scrub shielding the cave.

He could see Kelly's boat riding the shallows and Copper advancing down the sand toward it. Kelly stood up in his boat, holding something in his hand. As Copper reached the water's edge, Ryan realized with a shock that the fisherman was holding a rifle. Kelly took aim, and the crack of a shot reverberated around the bay.

Ryan saw Copper stagger, then turn to run. Another shot rang out and she fell. Behind Ryan, Selkie moaned in her sleep.

Copper lay on the shore, her sides heaving. She lifted her head, and it seemed as though she stared right at the cave. Anger churned inside Ryan at the sight of the stricken animal. That coward Kelly! Copper didn't have a chance to defend herself.

The seal struggled to rise, her flippers whacking the sand in distress. She cried out – a harsh, urgent sound. It was the call Ryan had heard the day Copper returned from her fishing trip and summoned her pup.

Selkie stirred and bleated. Ryan rummaged in his backpack and found a sandwich. He placed it in front of the seal and watched Selkie sniff it curiously, then gulp it down.

A guttural howl came from the beach, rose to a squeal, then stopped abruptly. Ryan sprang to the cave entrance. Kelly stood over Copper with a knife in his hand. Ryan watched in horror as the man bent over the dead seal, wielding his knife in long, slicing sweeps. Copper's coat began to fall away from her flesh.

Ryan turned away. Bile rose in his throat, and his head spun. He sank to his knees and laid his forehead on the cold rock floor. His breath was rapid and harsh, and his mouth tasted sour.

After a while, he lifted his head and gazed into Selkie's dark eyes. He moved close and gently pressed his nose to hers in the way he had seen Copper do. He felt the pup's warm breath on his cheeks, soft and soothing.

He stayed there for a moment, then sat back on his heels and took a deep breath. He felt drained yet clearheaded. He pulled his pack toward him and picked up his father's camera.

Ryan moved cautiously out of the cave and kneeled behind the brush. Kelly had nearly finished skinning the seal. Knife in hand, he stepped back to survey his work. Ryan focused the camera and pressed the shutter button. The *whirr* sounded loud in his ears.

Kelly bent forward to make a final slash, severing Copper's bloodstained pelt from her body. Again, Ryan pressed the shutter. Kelly dragged the seal's skin into the surf. The water turned deep red. Kelly heaved the skin into his boat. He rinsed his knife in the sea, sheathed it at his side, and turned to survey the bay.

Ryan kept still, holding his head low, his heart thudding loudly. He hoped Selkie would keep silent. Then he heard the sputter of the boat's motor. He watched Kelly steer the boat across the waves and disappear around the point.

Silence settled over the bay. Ryan stood up, trying to avoid looking at the abandoned carcass on the shore. He heard a scuffle and glanced down to see Selkie beside him. Snout pointing seaward, she sniffed the air, her nostrils flaring, and her whiskers twitching.

Mewling, she flapped over the sand toward the remains of her mother. Unsure of just what to do, Ryan followed.

When he reached the pup, she was snuffling over one of Copper's flippers. She nuzzled her mother's side, then raised her head and wailed a thin, high lament. Ryan shivered at the sound, and his own grief rose at the death of Copper.

A chill ocean breeze whipped across the bay, raising the hairs on Ryan's arms and legs. The tide began to creep in and swish around Copper's butchered body. Ryan longed to cover her, to clothe her in her warm sealskin. He remembered the selkie legend and how the fisherman stole the selkie woman's sealskin, preventing her from returning to the ocean.

Ryan stood in the swirling tide and vowed to find Copper's sealskin and return it to the ocean. The bite of the sea breeze brought tears to his eyes.

"And I'll take care of Selkie," he promised. He put his hand on the pup's head. "Come on, you've got to hide." But Selkie lay down beside her mother in the deepening water. Large gray-brown gulls circled and squawked overhead.

Ryan stood, undecided for a moment, then returned to the cave. He collected his backpack and walked back down to the water's edge. He took a sandwich from his pack and held it out to the pup.

At first, Selkie ignored him. Ryan waved the food near her nose, then drew it away. Selkie turned her head, watching his hand. Ryan dropped the sandwich in the sea. The pup's head darted forward, and she swallowed the snack.

Moving back, Ryan produced a packet of crackers. He held one out to Selkie. The pup followed him with her eyes, then slowly moved away from her mother's body and advanced toward Ryan. He rewarded her with a cracker and watched her devour it. Retreating up the beach, he held out another cracker. Gradually, he enticed the seal into the safety of the cave.

Inside, he stroked and soothed the pup, trying to get her to relax. Selkie stared back at him, alert and watchful. He felt in his pack, but he had exhausted his food supply. His fingers closed around his harmonica. He leaned back against the cave wall and blew softly into the instrument.

Outside, the waves slapped against the rocks. Ryan played a slow, wistful tune he remembered his father humming to him as a child. Closing his eyes, he felt the vibration of the harmonica against his lips and heard the reeds sing. He let the music wash over him.

A long time later, he lowered the harmonica and looked down at Selkie. Her eyes were closed and her body rose and fell in the rhythm of sleep. He took his sweater from his pack and bunched it near her head, then crept from the cave.

Once out of the cave, he sped across the bay, rounded the point, and scrambled up the rocks to the tunnel. He quickly wriggled through to the cliff side and slid over and down the boulder. Breathing heavily, he ran across the small inlet and clambered over the headland. Thankful that no one was on the beach to delay him, he hurried over the dunes toward his home.

Inside the kitchen, he flopped into a chair. Thoughts crowded his head. He would have to get Selkie away from the bay. It was too dangerous for her there. Kelly would go back for sure. The fisherman knew Copper had a pup, and he wouldn't pass up a chance for another sealskin.

Ryan decided to sleep in the cave with the pup that night. In the morning, he would try to get her to follow him out to sea. The ocean was cold now; he would need his wet suit and his snorkel gear. He rummaged in the fridge and stacked bread, ham, apples, and sardines on the table. He went to the freezer and took out the small fish he kept for bait; he would use them to lure Selkie into the ocean.

The back door swung open and Cilla breezed in. "Hi, Ryan. Mom's invited you to dinner." She stopped and eyed the pile of food. "What's all this for? Are you going away?"

"I was just about to have a snack," he said, feeling his cheeks flush.

"You can't eat all that at once," Cilla said. "You're hiding something."

"Don't be stupid," he said.

"Don't you call me stupid, you red-faced, lousy liar," Cilla accused. "What're you up to?"

"Nothing!"

Cilla folded her arms. "Tell me your secret or I'll tell Mom you look really sick and she'll hotfoot it over here with her medicine bag."

"You're a pain," Ryan sighed.

Cilla smiled.

Chapter 6

Ryan leaned back in his chair. "And that's everything." He felt relieved to have told someone about Selkie and the slaughter of Copper. "I'm going back to the bay soon. Tell your mother thanks for the dinner invitation, but say I can't come, because I'm working on a homework project."

"She'll be impressed," laughed Cilla. "I'll say I'm going to help you, then I can meet Selkie."

Ryan shook his head. "There's a couple of things I'd like for you to do."

Cilla frowned, torn between wanting to argue with him and curiosity. "What?"

"I need you to cover for me with your mom. I also need to know where Kelly lives so I can get Copper's sealskin and return it to the sea." He picked up a telephone book and flipped through the pages. "There're a few B. Kelly's listed, but I don't have time to find out which one is Ben Kelly. Will you call and say you're a visitor looking for your Uncle Ben?"

"Why don't you tell the police about Kelly and let them deal with him?"

"They won't take my word for what's happened," Ryan said. "They would waste time asking questions, and they would probably want to see the bay and what's left of Copper before they even started to check out Kelly."

"At least you could tell my parents," said Cilla. "They would believe you."

"Even if they did believe me, they would want to call the police. Adults think like that," he said. "Selkie is my responsibility. I have to make sure she's safe before other people are involved."

"I guess you're right."

"Promise me you won't tell anyone what's happened at the bay."

"All right." Cilla nodded. "I won't tell."

"And will you try to find out where Kelly lives?"

"Okay."

"Thanks," said Ryan. He stowed the supplies into his pack and filled a bottle with water.

"What are you going to do when Selkie starts crying for her mother's milk?" asked Cilla.

"She already lasts for days without a drink when Copper goes fishing."

"Maybe she'll get by on what she can find for herself," suggested Cilla.

"She'll have a fair chance of surviving if she can catch fish on her own," Ryan said, securing his sleeping bag to his pack with a bungee cord. "Come with me now and I'll show you the tunnel," he said, shouldering his gear. "If you come to the bay early enough tomorrow morning, you can help me get Selkie away."

They climbed over the headland and leaped onto the strip of sand. Ryan showed Cilla the concealed entrance. "On the other side you slide down the bank and go around the point to the bay."

"Take care of yourself – and Selkie," called Cilla as Ryan crawled into the shaft.

When he emerged from the tunnel, high tide had almost engulfed the point. Waves smashed against the foreshore as though the ocean was trying to swallow the land. He jumped from rock to rock, between the onrushing waves. His foot slipped on one boulder and his shin scraped down a sharp-edged rock. He waded through knee-deep breakers to the bay and searched the shore.

The beach was deserted. Waves covered the spot where he had last seen Copper; the ocean had claimed her body. Movement near the bluff drew his eye to the scrub. Selkie struggled through the brush and flapped toward the surf, bleating.

Ryan ran across the bay to her. She stopped at his approach, eyes wary, ready for flight. He slowed his pace and moved forward, calling softly.

He took a cracker from his bag and put it on the sand in front of the seal. She swallowed it eagerly, then sniffed his hand, looking for more. Ryan held out his pack and Selkie's snout wrinkled at the fishy smell of the bait inside.

"Follow me," he said and headed for the bluff, dragging the pack behind him. Selkie hesitated, then waddled after him.

An evening chill settled over the bay, and mist rolled in from the ocean. Shivering, Ryan entered the cave. His sweater lay on the floor where he had left it. He pulled it on and flapped his arms for warmth. Selkie watched his movements intently. He smiled; perhaps she thought he was about to sprout flippers.

In the fading light, he rationed out some food for himself and Selkie. The seal ate her share quickly.

"That's all you're getting," Ryan said. "We've got to make it last."

He unrolled his sleeping bag, spread it over the cave floor, and slipped into its warmth. Kelly isn't likely to come hunting at night, he thought, taking out his harmonica. Ryan played several fast numbers, the quick pace of his breathing warming him. Selkie lay beside him. She moved closer, propped her head on Ryan's stomach, and slept.

Ryan dozed fitfully, aware of his strange surroundings, the noises of the night, and the strong odor of the seal. Sometime in the early hours he woke to the sound of a night owl's cry. He felt cramped with Selkie leaning against him, so he eased himself from his sleeping bag. He stood up, flexed his legs, and moved quietly out of the cave.

Outside, the mist had cleared and stars sparkled in the night sky. A pale moon cast silhouettes of rocks and brush onto the bay. At sea, flickering navigation lights indicated the safe shipping lanes that skirted jagged outcrops.

Ryan saw the shadowy peak of an island rising from the black waters. A brilliant light shone out from the island's hillside to warn ships of the land ahead. The light swung from side to side, sweeping over the ocean and bay with its beam. A red beacon shone from the top of the island.

Tomorrow, I'll swim with Selkie out toward the island, Ryan thought. He hoped the pup would make its deserted shores her base until she was old enough to search for other seals. Ryan went back to the cave and snuggled into his sleeping bag. Selkie snorted and twitched in her sleep.

Ryan dreamed he was alone in the ocean, struggling to swim to a distant island. Waves swelled up and pushed against him without breaking. Arms flailing, he tried to force his way through the waves, which seemed to be covered with a thick skin. He scanned the sea, looking for Selkie. Where was she? He shouted her name, but no sound came. All he could hear was the cry of seagulls circling overhead.

He surfaced from the dream, struggling to free his arms from the tangled sleeping bag. Selkie pressed heavily against him, her body rising and falling like small ocean waves. Relieved, Ryan patted her head, and she raised sleepy eyes to gaze at him. She stretched and yawned. Her jaws opened wide to display her bright pink tongue and mouth.

"Phew!" Ryan choked as her fishy breath engulfed him.

Seagulls squawked outside. Ryan stumbled from the cave and watched as the sun began to climb above the horizon. The half-circle of flame shed a path of light across the ocean toward him. He shielded his eyes and looked seaward to the island he had decided to make his target.

"Hey there!" Cilla's voice called to him from the point. She ran across the bay toward him, her hair gleaming in the morning light. As she came near, the anxiety of his dream fell away. It would be all right if there were two of them to help Selkie.

"I brought you breakfast." Cilla put a bag on the sand and took out a package. "Hot dogs," she said, handing him one. "I told my mom we were going to explore around the coast today."

Ryan took a large bite of the warm food. "Thanks," he mumbled through the mouthful.

"One for each of us," said Cilla, clutching a second hot dog.

Drawn by the smell of food, Selkie emerged from the cave. She caught sight of Cilla and froze. Cilla also paused, her hand halfway to her mouth.

"Selkie!" Cilla exclaimed. "She's beautiful." She moved slowly toward the seal.

Uncertain, Selkie began to back away. Cilla made soothing noises as she held out her hot dog.

"Put it on the ground," Ryan said.

Cilla placed her hot dog in front of the seal and moved back a little. Selkie edged forward and began to gobble the food.

Cilla crept closer and kneeled beside Selkie, waiting until the pup finished. Then she extended her hand, and Selkie nuzzled her palm. Cilla moved her hand up and scratched behind the seal's ear. Selkie tolerated her attention for a moment then drew her head back.

"I'll get ready to lead her out to the island," Ryan said.

"It's a long way," said Cilla.

"The sooner we get going, the better." Ryan collected his gear in the cave and pulled on his wet suit. Then he picked up his pack with the fish he intended to use to lure Selkie. He strapped the pack to his chest and belted on his fishing knife.

"Time to go," he said.

Ryan carried his flippers, snorkel, and mask in one hand and waved a fish at Selkie with the other. The seal followed him as he moved toward the shore. At the water's edge, he rewarded Selkie with the fish and bent over to pull on his flippers.

"Not bad." Cilla nodded approval. "With your wet suit and flippers, Selkie will think you're one of her own kind."

"You try to scare her into the sea," said Ryan. He put on his snorkel and waded into the surf, flapping another fish at Selkie.

"I'll wait for you," Cilla called. She let out an ear-splitting screech, startling Selkie. As Cilla splashed and shouted in the shallows, Selkie scurried forward and launched into the surf, holding her snout up high.

Ryan headed out to sea, feeling the cold water creep into his wet suit. Selkie streaked past him, turned, and dived. Ryan felt a tug on his hand and the fish was gone. Clamping his teeth around the snorkel mouthpiece, he dipped his head below the surface. A dark shape glided beneath him, then doubled back to butt him playfully. Excitement flowed through him. He was swimming with Selkie! He was joining her in her world!

Ryan gave Selkie another fish then kicked his feet, feeling the flippers propel him forward. He raised his head to sight the island and swam toward it. Occasionally, he would see Selkie's head break the surface as she renewed her oxygen, then she would dive again. After a few minutes, she would reappear some distance from where he had last seen her. She never left him for long. Sometimes he felt her nudge his stomach or chest, searching for more fish.

Treading water for a moment, Ryan looked back to the bay. He waved, and Cilla swung both arms in acknowledgment. He felt good knowing she was there. He turned and continued toward the island.

As he swam farther out, the sea roughened, slapping against him and tossing him around like a piece of driftwood. A huge wave cascaded over him, sweeping him sideways and dislodging his mask. He grabbed at his mask and looked around for Selkie.

She surfaced close to him, rolled over, and with a flick of her rear flippers, she dived again. Moments later the sea boiled and she burst upward, only to sink back under the water as though something dragged at her from the ocean.

In that brief glimpse, Ryan saw her wild-eyed stare and the net around her head. He adjusted his mask and snorkel, loosened his knife from its sheath, and dived. The water churned around Selkie as she struggled to free herself from a discarded fishing net. Her desperate efforts wound the net tighter around her body.

Ryan grabbed the net at the back of Selkie's neck, slid his knife behind the weave, and sliced through the nylon. The net fell away from her head. His snorkel filling with water and his lungs straining, Ryan kicked quickly upward. He surfaced, cleared his snorkel, drew a deep breath, then dived again.

He tugged at the net trapping Selkie's front flippers and cut it. One flipper sprang out, and he turned to the other, conscious of the tightness in his chest. Within seconds, the net slackened and

Selkie twisted free. She flicked her body toward the surface, her rear flippers slapping hard into Ryan's face. He gasped and breathed in water. Thrashing wildly, he clawed upward.

Ryan reached the surface and lay with his chin barely cresting the water, his body limp. Something jolted into him. A nose nudged his face, and he stared into Selkie's dark eyes.

He breathed in and choked. Gasping, he drew a shallow breath, aware of a deep ache in his chest. He coughed up salt water, the brackish taste souring his throat. Selkie swam ahead a little, then circled back and butted into him.

"Leave me alone," he croaked. She pushed her snout into his shoulder, then swam forward again, pausing to look back at him.

"Okay, okay." Ryan forced his legs to kick and thrust him along in Selkie's wake. The pup was headed back toward the safety of the bay.

Ryan followed her, lifting his arms mechanically. He raised his head once and saw the distant figure of Cilla on the beach. A bundle of kelp tangled around his legs. He kicked it away and battled on through the swelling sea. Selkie stayed close to him until they reached the breakers, then she swam ahead. He rode in with the waves until one surged over him, rolled him under, then pitched him into the shallows, where he lay gasping.

Ryan felt strong arms encircle him. Cilla tugged him away from the water's edge and propped him into a sitting position. She kneeled behind him to support him. Gradually, the pounding in his head eased and his breathing slowed. "Thanks," he said.

"What happened out there?" Cilla asked.

"Selkie got tangled in an old net, and it nearly drowned both of us." Ryan stood up. "I'm too beat to swim to the island now. I'll have to get Dad's boat and take her there."

"Do you think she'll stay on the island?" asked Cilla. "She came straight back to the bay when she got scared."

"I'll have to get Copper's sealskin to take with us," he answered. "Copper's scent should keep Selkie there."

"I called each B. Kelly in the phone book," said Cilla. "One grumpy guy said he was Ben Kelly and was a fisherman. But he said he didn't have a niece, nor did he want one."

"Where does he live?"

"His address was in the phone book." Cilla took a scrap of paper from her pocket and handed it to Ryan. "He lives at 97 Seaview Road. That's down the coast road, past where we turn into Ocean Vista."

"Will you stay here with Selkie while I get the sealskin?"

"Sure. I told my mom we would both be away all day."

"There's a can of sardines in my backpack," Ryan said. "Use them to coax her into the cave. Keep out of sight with her until I come back with the boat."

Ryan went to the cave, peeled off his wet suit, and tugged on his dry clothes. He hurried across the bay, toward the point, where he turned to wave to Cilla. Selkie was basking on a rock next to his friend, unaware of any danger.

Chapter 7

Back at home, Ryan loaded gas and supplies into the boat. He pushed aside a twinge of guilt about taking the dinghy out. He had to get Selkie away from the bay.

He grabbed some bungee cords and wheeled his bike down the driveway. He glanced over at Cilla's house and was thankful no one was in sight.

Cycling along the coast road, Ryan thought about his failed attempt to help Selkie escape. He was unsure whether his present plan would succeed, but he couldn't abandon her. She had already lost her mother, and he was certain she wouldn't survive without him.

A weather-beaten sign, almost hidden by long grass, pointed to Seaview Road. No houses were visible from the main road. Ryan hid his bike in a grass-covered ditch and walked down the gravel road leading to the ocean.

Farther along, an abandoned cottage stood with its door opening into an empty shell. At the end of the road, Ryan came to the only other house, an old weathered bungalow set back among the trees.

Ryan crouched and moved along the boundary hedge until he came level with an open window. He heard a man speaking and recognized Kelly's voice. From the fisherman's one-way conversation, Ryan guessed he was making a phone call.

"Yeah, it's a good skin, no marks on it. I've got it pegged out in the yard to dry. What's your offer?" There was a pause while Kelly listened. "No way, that's not enough. This season's lousy fish catch has left me up to my eyeballs in debt." Silence again. "Listen, there's a heavy fine for killing a seal. The hide has to be worth the risk I'm taking." Kelly baited another hook. "Look, I'll sweeten the deal. There's also a seal pup's skin I can get if you name a good price." Kelly waited for a reply. "That's better," he said, sounding pleased with the new deal. "I'll get some more ammunition, then I'll go hunt for the pup."

Kelly replaced the receiver, and after a few moments, a truck's engine whirred and sputtered. The motor revved to a throaty roar, and Ryan saw Kelly drive down the access road in a battered pickup truck.

Ryan made his way to the rear of the house and stopped. Copper's skin was stretched out and tethered to pegs driven into the ground.

Beads of moisture rose to the surface of the upturned skin, drawn out by the late afternoon sun. Ryan kneeled down beside the hide. The strong seal smell filled his nostrils and caught in the back of his throat. He bent forward and worked to free Copper's hide. The skin sagged in the middle as he released one corner. He sat back on his heels and wiped his forehead with his hand.

"You're going back to where you belong," Ryan said, working quickly to free the remainder of Copper's hide. He folded the thick pelt into a bundle and secured it between his shoulders with the bungee cords he had brought from home. It weighed heavily on his back. He hurried along the side of Kelly's house and sprinted down the gravel road to the ditch where he had hidden his bike.

If Kelly sees me, I'm in big trouble, he thought. Head down and legs pumping, he rode along the main road. Sweat trickled between his shoulder blades from the heat of Copper's pelt. Only a few cars passed him before he reached the Ocean Vista turnoff. With a sigh of relief, he headed toward the beach and coasted home, keeping an eye out for Cilla's parents.

Inside the boat shed, he eased Copper's hide from his shoulders and placed it in the bottom of the dinghy. He took his father's binoculars from a shelf, slung them around his neck, then dragged the boat over the sand to the ocean.

He launched the boat into the surf, riding the waves past the headland and motoring on toward the bay. He felt drowsy as rays from the sinking sun slanted across him. His eyelids closed and he shook himself awake. He couldn't rest until he had Selkie safe on the island.

The boat rounded the point leading into the bay, and Ryan scanned the empty stretch of sand. He beached the dinghy and ran toward the bluff.

"Cilla, I'm back," he called, bending down to the cave entrance.

Scuffling sounded inside, then Cilla's muffled voice answered, "Coming." She scrambled out and stretched. "Selkie makes a great pillow," she said. "Too bad about her body odor, though. It really knocks you out."

Ryan grinned as the seal emerged from the cave, blinking in the light. "What a lazy pair," he said.

"While I've been risking life and limb, you two have been napping."

"Did you find Copper's skin?"

"Sure did. But Kelly's going to be coming after Selkie soon."

Cilla watched the seal flap over the sand toward the ocean. "We'll have to get her away from here fast," she said.

"I'll have to get my things together." Ryan entered the cave, filled his backpack, and rolled up his sleeping bag.

Cilla helped him carry his gear down to the dinghy. The receding tide had left the boat stuck in the sand. He shoved it into the waves. Curious, Selkie joined him in the water and swam between his legs.

"Wait for me," Cilla called.

"Cilla, you can't come," said Ryan.

"But you're always leaving me behind," she protested.

"I need you to cover for me at your house," Ryan said.

Selkie nudged the backs of Ryan's legs. "Help me get her over the side," he said. "We've got to get her in the first time or she'll take off."

He bent over and stroked Selkie's underbelly. Cilla leaned forward and clasped Ryan's wrists in a cradle under the seal.

"One, two, heave!" They locked their arms, straightened their legs, and lifted Selkie into the boat. The dinghy rocked as the startled seal slid along the bottom.

Ryan scrambled into the dinghy, put on his life jacket, and pulled the starter cord. "Don't tell anyone where I've gone," he said. "I want to find a safe spot for Selkie first."

Ryan steered the boat through the breakers. He turned to look at Cilla standing knee-deep in the water. She raised her hand to wave, and Ryan fought an impulse to turn around and go back.

"Go home now, before Kelly comes," he shouted to her.

Cilla moved back, stopped at the water's edge to wave once more, then sprinted across the sand. She climbed over the rocks around the point and, with a final wave, disappeared from sight.

Ryan shivered as the evening wind tugged at him. He looked at Selkie slumped in the bottom of the boat. Her sides heaved, and she raised her dejected eyes to him. He leaned forward and pushed Copper's pelt toward her.

The seal's nostrils flared as the sharp aroma of the hide reached her. She arched her neck and mewled. Struggling forward, she nudged the pelt with her nose. A shudder rippled down her body, and she laid her head on her mother's fur.

Ryan glanced at the empty ocean. Good. Kelly hadn't reached the bay yet.

"You're going to be safe now, Selkie," he said. Kelly wouldn't find any sign of the seal when he got to the bay. Then Ryan remembered the dinghy getting stuck in the sand. When he had pushed the boat into the sea, he had left tracks and footprints. It was too late to go back and wipe out his traces. Kelly would know someone had been there.

Ryan didn't want to consider what would happen if Kelly linked him with the seals and the disappearance of the sealskin. If the fisherman remembered him, Ryan hoped Kelly would think he had only gone back to the bay to swim.

Ryan focused on the island. It rose from the ocean like a fortress. The sea darkened to an emerald green as the waters deepened. A shaft of light from the last rays of the sun flecked the underside of a curling wave a lighter green, and the dinghy plowed through the swelling ocean.

Chapter 8

Ryan guided the dinghy toward the island. The rotating navigation light on the hillside swung its beam across the ocean, and Ryan steered the boat past a craggy outcrop at the base of the island. Waves crashed over the rocks in an explosion of white foam.

Farther around the island, a gap in the rocks opened onto a small inlet. Ryan maneuvered the boat toward the shore, leaped out, and dragged it high up on the sand. He reached into the dinghy and lifted Selkie's head from her mother's hide.

"Come on, girl," he said. "We need to find some shelter."

Ryan hauled out Copper's pelt and leaned on the edge of the boat, tipping it until Selkie rolled toward him. She half-scrambled, half-fell onto the sand. He picked up the sealskin and stumbled up the beach with Selkie waddling behind.

A sweep of light spread out from the hillside and lit up the inlet. Ryan saw an uprooted tree lying beyond the high-tide line of broken shells. The trunk jutted out at an angle from the base of the hill.

"This will do," he said, spreading Copper's skin in the sheltered V between the bank and the fallen tree. Selkie flopped onto the skin and nuzzled into the fur.

Ryan returned to the dinghy and dug the boat's anchor into the sand. Then he climbed the rocks shielding the inlet. The navigation light sent a shaft of light across the empty ocean. For tonight, they were safe.

He went back to the dinghy, took out his sleeping bag and backpack, and made his way back to the fallen tree. Ryan stretched out beside Selkie, welcoming her warmth in spite of her strong animal smell.

He slept heavily, without dreaming. He awoke at dawn, confused, wondering for a moment where he was. Then the memory of Copper's slaughter and his journey to the island flooded back.

Selkie lay sleeping beside him with her flippers tucked under her plump body. She breathed through her nose, and Ryan smiled as her spiky whiskers rose and fell with each breath. He remembered the joy of swimming with her and how she had transformed from an awkward land creature into a sleek ocean acrobat.

Ryan turned over and looked up at a cheerless sky. It spread overhead like a dome and curved down to merge with the gray ocean. A faint circle of light tried to force its way through the blanket of cloud. Ryan's stomach rumbled, reminding him that he hadn't eaten for a long time.

He took a sandwich from his backpack and checked over his supplies. A few apples, some sandwiches, and a packet of crackers remained, plus a container of water still in the boat. He would survive, but he worried about Selkie. The seal stirred, wrinkled her nose, and bleated.

"Good morning, sleepyhead," said Ryan. He opened the crackers and gave Selkie one. "That's all for now. We need to go fishing for your breakfast."

Ryan made his way down to the beach with Selkie scurrying and snuffling along behind him. His fishing gear still lay in the bottom of the dinghy, where he'd left it during his hurried arrival home from the bay earlier in the week.

He took his rod and quickly pried a few shellfish off the rocks by the dinghy. He threaded their flesh onto a hook, balanced on a rock, and cast his line into the surf. He soon felt a tug on his line and reeled it in, but the fish had escaped.

Ryan baited his hook again and cast his line. This time he caught a small fish, which he unhooked and held out to Selkie. She swallowed it whole, then leaned forward on her front flippers, watching him expectantly. Ryan caught three more fish, which Selkie gulped down, then she pushed her snout into his hand, searching for more.

"Greedy little beast," Ryan said.

He felt hot and sticky and stripped off his shirt. He clambered down the rocks and lowered himself into the water. To his delight, the seal joined him.

He lay on his back the way he had seen Copper do, and Selkie glided over to him, placing her snout on his chest. Then she nudged him away and spiraled into the sea. Ryan rolled over and saw Selkie's dark shape twist and turn beneath him. A school of small fish swam nearby, and Selkie darted among them. She surfaced close to Ryan with her mouth full.

"You sly thing, you knew how to catch fish all along," he laughed. "You can catch your own food from now on."

It pleased Ryan that Selkie was no longer dependent on him for her survival. But she still needed a base on land, and that would make her vulnerable when Kelly came hunting for her. At the thought of Kelly, Ryan turned and swam for shore. The dinghy made them easy to spot. He would have to hide it.

On the beach, he pulled the boat behind a curve of rocks and brushed away the trail with a branch from the fallen tree. Although the dinghy was shielded from view, Ryan realized that a quick escape was now impossible. He and Selkie could become trapped in the inlet. He needed to explore the small island for an escape route.

Selkie shook the water from her coat and followed him up the beach. She sat on her mother's pelt, grooming herself. Ryan watched her easily twist her head to get to the hard-to-reach parts of her body. Tired from her fishing trip, she yawned and lay down, closing her eyes.

Ryan took the binoculars from his pack. He looked up at the steep hill and saw twisted tree trunks clinging to the side with corkscrew branches grasping for the sky. A path wound up the hill, and he clambered over boulders toward it. He climbed upward, using branches as handholds and jutting rocks as steps.

The sun came out and shone on Ryan's back, and sweat trickled down between his shoulders. He steadied himself against a bank and wiped his forehead. A fly buzzed around him. Irritated, he swatted at it and felt his foot slide. He regained his footing and continued upward.

The roar of the ocean receded as he climbed up the path. His thighs began to ache and his chest felt tight. He cleared his throat to relieve the metallic taste in his mouth. A flock of sparrows rose from a bush in a flutter of wings. Ryan glanced down and saw the inlet far below. The dinghy looked like a toy boat, and he could just make out Selkie curled up behind the tree.

The path wound through a patch of bushes. Silence encompassed Ryan, and it seemed as if he had entered a timeless place that hadn't been disturbed for ages. It felt protective, like a sanctuary. Maybe a long time ago the island had given shelter to shipwrecked sailors.

The path veered out again to overlook the ocean. Beside the path, the huge navigation light sat motionless against the hill like a sleeping guardian. It must work the same way as a security light, thought Ryan, with sensors that activated the light when dusk fell.

The path narrowed and wound higher and higher. Ryan kept climbing, hugging the hillside. His foot caught on a tree root, throwing him off balance. He stumbled sideways, and the path's edge crumbled beneath his shoe. Rubble cascaded down, and he pulled back against the hill. Not daring to look down, he trudged on.

Finally, the path opened on an expanse of barren ground at the summit. Dusty soil swirled in the breeze, coating the tufts of wind-burned grass with a fine powder. In the middle of the clearing, a beacon with four red lights encased in mesh sat on top of a wooden pole.

Ryan walked to the far side of the summit and looked down. An almost sheer cliff descended to the sea. He moved around the edge of the hilltop, searching for an escape route. A landslide blocked one side, and other parts of the hill were covered in dense bushes or jagged boulders. Rabbit burrows pockmarked the occasional grassy hump. The path Ryan had come up seemed to be the only access. The island was both a refuge and a prison.

Wondering if his absence had been detected, he raised his binoculars and looked toward Ocean Vista, focusing on Cilla's house. He felt less alone knowing her place was within sight, although there was no practical way he could attract her attention from this distance.

The windows of his own house looked blank, and Ryan noticed patches of moss growing on the roof. Weeds had regained control of the garden he had worked on with his mother before she went away. He thought about how fractured his family life had become. It was like a seawall that had been battered by too many waves and had finally crumbled. After talking with his father, Ryan understood the stresses that caused the damage, but he had no idea if the rift could be mended.

He swung the binoculars over the headland and to the deserted bay. Farther around the mainland, Ryan spotted Kelly's fishing boat moving along the coast. The fisherman was searching for the seal pup in the wrong place, but it was only a matter of time before he turned his attention to the island.

It worried Ryan that Selkie was easy prey on land. The sea held her greatest prospect of survival. In the ocean she could move out of reach in a flash.

He started down the path. His momentum propelled him speedily along, his feet slipping and sliding on the stony soil. He fell once, leaped up, and kept going.

Heart pounding, Ryan reached the base of the hill and jumped over the boulders. He saw Selkie by the tidemark of broken shells, making her way toward the ocean.

"Hey! Wait for me," he called.

Selkie paused and looked back at him, her head tilted to one side. Beyond the breakers, Ryan saw a dark shape dive beneath the water and resurface a few moments later. That can't be a dolphin, he thought. They don't usually swim alone. He focused the binoculars on the bullet-shaped head skimming the waves.

"It's a seal!" he shouted.

He ran to the boat and put on his wet suit, snorkel, and mask. If he could lead Selkie out to the other seal, it might accept her as a companion. Ryan entered the shallows, with Selkie flapping along beside him. They moved into deeper waters, the cold current seeping into Ryan's wet suit.

Selkie stayed with him until she caught sight of a school of fish and snaked after them. He looked around for the other seal and spotted it a short distance away. Selkie's head crested a wave, and Ryan beat the water with his hands to attract her attention. She skimmed toward him, happy to join in a new game. Drawn by the activity, the other seal approached them. As it came closer, Ryan thought it looked longer than a fur seal. It moved differently, too. Its hind end swayed in a sculling motion. Selkie swam using her front flippers.

Selkie came alongside Ryan and barked a greeting to the advancing seal. With its large, sloping head, it had an almost serpentine appearance. As it plunged toward them, Ryan caught a glimpse of spots glistening on its hide.

Ryan positioned his mask to watch the two seals meet underwater. The water churned below him, and bubbles disturbed his vision. Then he saw Selkie streak past with the other seal close behind. Horrified, Ryan realized it was attacking Selkie. Of course! The seal had spots; it must be a leopard seal. He had led Selkie to her enemy!

Ryan released the knife at his side. Beneath him, Selkie turned and twisted, rapidly changing direction as she tried to escape. She spiraled up toward Ryan. As the leopard seal closed in, Ryan flicked his knife up. The knife cut into the seal's hide as the predator flashed past, its momentum knocking the knife from his hand.

The leopard seal faltered, its hind flippers thrashing the water as it turned toward Ryan. Blood trickled from a gash in its side as the seal wavered, altered direction, and dived. Numb with shock, Ryan saw it surface farther out at sea, then it disappeared from sight.

Beside him, Selkie floundered in distress. A stream of blood spread out from her side where the leopard seal had bitten her. Ryan reached out to Selkie. "Hang in there," he urged. Struggling to keep afloat, he pushed Selkie toward the island.

While at sea, they had drifted, and they now approached a cove farther around the island from the inlet. As they neared the shore, a wave swept Selkie away from Ryan and dashed her against rocks. She collapsed back into the water and began to sink. Struggling to reach her, Ryan saw another swell lift her up and thrust her between the rocks. He reached the rocks and hauled himself up. Selkie lay awkwardly, blood trickling from her side.

"You can't stay here," Ryan said. "You'll get washed back out to sea." Trying to avoid hurting her, he nudged and prodded her forward. Selkie heaved herself over the rocks and flopped down in a patch of weathered grass sheltered by the cove.

Ryan crouched beside her and examined her side. The leopard seal had bitten into Selkie's flesh, but Ryan had intervened before it could do serious injury. He could see the blood already beginning to congeal and the seal's blubber folding around the wound. The pup would need to rest quietly for a while, though.

Ryan looked up at the hillside. From his earlier survey of the island, he guessed the inlet was not that far away. He didn't think it would take him long to clamber around the base of the island and bring back their supplies.

Selkie lay with her head stretched out and her eyes half-closed. "Stay there, girl," Ryan said and moved away. The afternoon sun had vanished behind the clouds, and Ryan shivered as he climbed over the rocks. His wet suit clung to his body, hampering his movements. He tried to move as quickly as possible, aware that time was running out for Selkie's escape.

He reached the rocks overlooking the inlet, jumped down, and hurried to the fallen tree. His backpack lay beside the mother seal's pelt. Ryan stroked the soft fur. "I'm doing my best to look after her, Copper," he said.

He stripped off his wet suit, changed into his clothes, and picked up his backpack containing their meager supplies. The seawater he had swallowed while helping Selkie had left him with a husky throat and an acrid taste in his mouth. As Ryan knelt by the dinghy to get the water bottle, he heard a boat motor approaching from the direction of the mainland.

"Kelly," he groaned. "It must be Kelly."

Chapter 9

Ryan glanced around the inlet. It would be useless to hide here. He would soon be discovered. He reached into the dinghy and shoved the water container in his pack. He caught sight of a distress flare his father kept in the boat and grabbed it.

The sound of the boat engine drew near. He raced across the sand and scrambled over the rocks leading back to Selkie. Between a gap in the rocks he watched as the boat skirted the outcrop and approached the inlet.

Kelly stood at the wheel of the boat, guiding it toward shore. The fisherman cut the motor and it sputtered and died. Ryan's ears ached in the silence that followed, and he swallowed to ease a tickle in the back of his throat. It would be only a matter of minutes before Kelly found his boat and began searching for him.

Ryan looked up at the hill. The only way out was to climb, and even then there was no escape. At least it would buy some time, he thought. He shouldered his pack and leaped over boulders toward the path winding up to the summit.

He clambered up the hillside, grabbing at branches for support. As he hauled himself up and over the thick roots of an ancient tree, he glanced down at the inlet.

Kelly was standing beside the fallen tree, looking at Copper's pelt. Ryan realized the fisherman would guess that whoever was on the island also knew he had slaughtered the seal. Kelly gazed across the sand at Ryan's footprints leading to the rocks. He moved to follow the tracks.

If he keeps going around the base of the island he'll find Selkie's cove! thought Ryan. He had to draw Kelly away. He picked up a rock and heaved it. It bounced off the side of the hill, dislodging a clod of dirt and small stones, which clattered down the hillside.

Kelly looked up and Ryan allowed him to catch a glimpse of his face before he pulled back. He heard the fisherman's boots scrape on the rocks at the bottom of the hill. Kelly was coming after him.

Ryan slipped out from behind the tree and entered the sheltered patch of bush along the path. He had no idea what to do next, but he knew that he must lead Kelly away from Selkie. He kept climbing, his heart thudding and his throat burning.

The path wound outward and brought him alongside the navigation light. Ryan stopped and stared at it. It would soon be dusk, and the light would sweep the island and its waters, making it easier for Kelly to spot Selkie.

Ryan found a sturdy branch and swung at the thick glass protecting the light. A small crack spread across the curved shield. He swung again and a shower of glass exploded from the light. A bulb sat in the middle surrounded by a reflector. He rammed the end of the branch into the bulb, shattering it.

Ryan heard some branches crack below him and guessed Kelly had made it nearly halfway up the hill. That gave Ryan a good lead. He hastened up the narrowing path toward the hilltop, pushing his aching legs onward.

He staggered into the summit clearing and dropped to his knees, gasping for breath. He slid off his pack, pulled out the water container and took a long swig. Water trickled from the edges of his mouth and down his neck.

Ryan took the binoculars from the pack and climbed to his feet. The Ocean Vista houses stood out like a haven. He saw a plume of smoke rise from the chimney of Cilla's house. Cilla must be at home now, Ryan realized. He grabbed the distress flare container from his pack, pulled off the cap, and shook out the flare. Holding it upright, Ryan released the safety pin and flicked off the cap.

The flare ignited and rocketed upward, flame shooting from the end. It soared high into the sky before a small parachute opened and a cloud of red smoke billowed out. He knew Cilla probably wouldn't see it, but it was his only hope. Time seemed to stop while the parachute hovered over the island, then it faltered and fell, trailing its fading signal.

He heard Kelly approach the summit and turned to face him. The fisherman stumbled into the clearing. Recognition flickered as he glared at Ryan. "You're playing a dangerous game, boy."

"What do you mean?"

"Don't mess with me! Did you really think you would get away with stealing my sealskin so you could make some easy money?"

Ryan's thoughts raced. He was surprised by Kelly's accusation that he had taken Copper's skin to sell for himself, but it gave him a chance to gain more time for Selkie.

Kelly stood watching Ryan intently. "You know where the seal pup is, too, don't you?"

"She's gone," said Ryan. "Out to sea."

"Don't lie to me." Kelly moved closer and gripped Ryan's arm. "Take me to her. Now!"

Ryan looked defiantly at the older man. "What's in it for me if I show you where to find the pup?"

Kelly stroked his chin. "Fifty bucks."

Ryan shook his head. "Eighty."

"You're hardly in a position to bargain," Kelly said. "Sixty dollars, and that's final."

Ryan nodded.

"Let's get a move on, then," said Kelly. "It'll be dark soon."

Ryan bent to pick up his pack and Kelly stepped on his hand. "Leave it," he said.

"There's food in there for the seal," said Ryan, flexing his crushed fingers. "It will make it easier for us to get near her."

"Okay, pick it up," said Kelly. "Let's go."

On the way down the hill, Ryan considered ways he could escape, although he knew it was unlikely he could shake off the fisherman. Even if he did manage to get away from him, where could he go? The only exit was by sea. And Ryan knew he wouldn't last very long in the ocean without his wet suit.

Near the bottom of the hill, a rabbit darted out from a clump of grass and shot across the path, in front of Kelly. The fisherman stumbled and Ryan sprang forward.

"No you don't." Kelly grabbed Ryan's pack. Ryan felt himself dragged backward.

"Don't give me any trouble, got it?" said Kelly, grabbing his arm. He held on to Ryan until they reached the bottom of the path, then he shoved him over the boulders.

"Get that sealskin and put it over in my boat," he ordered.

Fighting back his anger, Ryan picked up Copper's pelt and carried it down the beach. Kelly reached into his boat and took out his rifle.

"You can't shoot her," said Ryan. "She's holed up in a cove under a cliff. A rifle shot could ricochet back on us."

"Then I'll have to club her, just like the old sealers," said Kelly, picking up a thick branch with a gnarled end. He stowed the rifle back in the boat and took out a large flashlight, which he shone in Ryan's face. "Well, where do we go?"

Ryan turned away from the light, feeling sick with defeat. Kelly had already sailed around the mainland side of the inlet and would know the seal was not in that direction. There was no other option but to take him over the rocks to the cove.

"This way," he said.

A biting wind whipped foam into the air, and evening clouds darkened the ocean. Ryan stumbled over the rocks, taking as long as he possibly could. Kelly followed him, the light from his flashlight dancing across shallow pools and sending crabs scuttling for cover.

When they reached the cove, Ryan turned to Kelly. He had a desperate urge to try to overpower him. But he knew that one blow from the heavy club the fisherman carried would knock him senseless. "We're here," Ryan said.

Kelly shone his flashlight into the dark recesses of the cove. The beam traveled over a dark hump pressed against a rock. Ryan's heart ached at the sight of Selkie cowering from the light. The only thing he could do for her now was to stall Kelly.

"I'll draw her out from the cliff," Ryan said. He moved toward Selkie and kneeled down beside her. "There, girl," he said, stroking her head. "Take it easy now."

He took off his pack and found a sandwich. He offered it to Selkie, the stale bread crumbling in his fingers. The seal gulped it down and snuffled his hand, searching for more food. He could see that her side had begun to heal. It was so unjust that she had survived an attack from her natural enemy only to be trapped by a lowlife like Kelly.

The fisherman edged forward. "Bring her out a bit farther so I can get a clear swing at her," he said, gripping the club. Selkie tossed her head and barked as he moved near.

Ryan stood up and faced Kelly. "Do your own dirty work," he said.

"What's the matter?" sneered Kelly. "Haven't got the stomach for it?" He stepped forward, swinging the club in his hand.

Above the sound of the surf breaking on the rocks, Ryan heard the high whine of another boat.

Kelly turned off the flashlight. "Get back out of sight," he said. "And don't make a sound." Ryan felt the sharp point of a knife jab into his side.

A shore patrol boat rounded the island, its powerful searchlight probing the waters and shoreline. The beam passed over the rocks and swung toward the cove. Kelly moved back, stumbling over Selkie. She snarled, reared up, and lunged at him, her teeth slashing into his thigh. Kelly dropped his knife and yelled.

"What's going on there?" demanded the patrol boat captain, aiming the searchlight into the cove.

Selkie hung on to Kelly, shaking her head back and forth like a dog holding a rabbit. The fisherman struck her on the head and pulled free. Howling with pain and rage, he splashed through the water toward the patrol boat.

"You're just in time," he called. "I saw this kid in the cove while I was out fishing. I beached my boat and climbed around to see what he was up to." He pointed a finger at Ryan. "He pulled a knife on me."

"Don't believe him," shouted Ryan. "He was going to slaughter this seal."

"The kid's just trying to save his own hide," said Kelly, climbing into the patrol boat. "I got here just in time to keep him from killing the pup."

"He's lying!" shouted Ryan.

"Come on, son," called the captain. "You'll have to come back with us so we can sort all this out."

Ryan dropped to his knees and put his arms around Selkie. "At least you're safe," he said. He had kept his promise to Copper. "Look in his boat at the inlet!" he shouted. "He's got a sealskin in it." Ryan grabbed his pack and pulled out his father's camera. "And I can prove how he got it," he yelled, wading through the water to the patrol boat. "I've got photos of him slaughtering the seal and skinning her." A crew member leaned over and helped Ryan climb into the boat. Kelly glared at him.

"Did you see my distress flare?" Ryan asked the captain. "Is that what made you come?"

"We received a report of a flare in this area," the captain answered. "We noticed the navigation light was out and guessed something was happening on the island."

The patrol boat motored into the inlet. A crew member went over to Kelly's boat and shone a flashlight in the bottom. "The boy's right," he said. "There's a sealskin here."

The captain turned to Kelly. "We're confiscating your boat." A crew member hooked a towrope onto the bow of Kelly's boat.

"Can I follow you in my father's dinghy?" Ryan asked the captain.

The captain nodded and Ryan waded ashore. He pushed the dinghy toward the surf and climbed on board. The patrol boat skirted the island, with Kelly's boat trailing behind it.

Ryan followed, relieved to be going home. A deep tiredness settled over him. His every action seemed to happen without thought or feeling, as though he moved on autopilot. He longed to lie down in a warm bed and sleep.

Chapter 10

The lights of Ocean Vista flickered through the mist as the patrol boat towed Kelly's boat toward a jetty. Several police officers helped dock both boats and took Kelly into custody.

Ryan coasted into the jetty and flung a rope to a man who caught it and tied it around a bollard. The man bent down and held out a hand. Looking up, Ryan was surprised to see it was his father.

"I'm so relieved that you're all right, Ryan," his father said.

Ryan took his father's hand. He climbed onto the jetty and felt it shake beneath him as footsteps pounded along the boards. Cilla burst out of the mist and flung herself at Ryan. He reeled back against the bollard, feeling her arms encircle him. She made a sound like a sob mixed with a chuckle. "You smell bad," she said.

He laughed and held her away from him. "Same old Cilla." He grinned. "Were you the one who saw my distress flare?"

"No, it was Dad. He had just come home when he saw the flare. I heard him phone the shore patrol and I realized you must be in trouble." Cilla faltered. "I had to tell my dad about Kelly and the seals. He called the police, and we've all been waiting, hoping the patrol boat would find you."

"It's okay. Help came just in time," said Ryan.

"When I found you and the boat gone I was worried," Ryan's father said. "I went to the

Hansens', and Cilla told me what you had gone through." He put his arm around Ryan's shoulders. "You've been very brave, Ryan, but you took an awful risk."

"I had to, Dad," Ryan said. "Selkie really needed my help."

"Is she safe?" asked Cilla.

"I think so," said Ryan.

A police officer approached Ryan. "We'll need a statement from you," he said.

"He needs warm clothes and food first," Ryan's father said. "You can talk to him at our house in an hour." The police officer nodded in agreement.

Cilla tugged at Ryan's arm. "Come on," she said.

As they walked home, his father said, "Your mother phoned earlier, and I told her what little I knew. She was very upset."

"I didn't mean to cause so much trouble, Dad."

"I know you wanted to protect the seal, but you shouldn't have taken the boat out on your own again," his father said. "But I guess we've both made some mistakes. I haven't been totally honest with you, either."

Ryan stared at his father in amazement. "What do you mean?"

"My business took me to the area where your grandma lives," he replied. "I arranged to see your mother. I didn't tell you, because I didn't want to get your hopes up if nothing came of the visit."

That explained why he was so tense about going away, thought Ryan. "How is Mom?"

"She's fine," his father said. "We talked a lot. I'll tell you about it later."

At home, Ryan stood under the shower for a long time, letting the water flow over him. His skin tingled as warmth slowly returned to his body. The phone rang as he was dressing. He heard his father speak for a moment, then call up to him, "Ryan, it's your mother."

In the kitchen, Cilla and his father were busy preparing a meal. Ryan picked up the phone. "Hello? Mom?"

"Ryan! Are you all right?"

His mother's voice sounded so full of concern, Ryan found it difficult to speak at first. He longed to see her again. "I'm fine, Mom," he finally managed to reply.

"That's a relief," she said. "Ryan, no matter what has happened, we can work it out."

"It's a long story."

"Don't worry about it right now. You sound very tired," she said. "I'll come home tomorrow and we can talk then."

"That'll be great," he said. He wanted to ask if that meant she was coming home to stay, but he didn't know if he could cope with the answer right then. "How is Grandma?"

"She's well enough now to manage with some help from her neighbor."

"That's good," said Ryan.

"I'll see you tomorrow," his mother said. "I love you, Ryan."

"I love you, too," answered Ryan, and he replaced the receiver.

Cilla placed a plate piled with food in front of him and sat on the opposite side of the table with a cup of cocoa. Two police officers came, and in between bites, Ryan told them about the slaughter of Copper and the events that followed.

As the warmth of the kitchen and the food sank in, a deep weariness enveloped him. His own voice sounded distant and his words slurred.

The police officers stood up. "That's enough for tonight," said one. "Later, when Kelly is in court, you'll have to repeat your story to the judge."

Ryan remembered Copper's pelt. "Can I have the sealskin back?" he asked. "I promised to return it to the sea."

"We'll need it as evidence," said a police officer. "But the judge will consider your request."

Ryan woke to daylight streaming through the bedroom curtains. He remembered that his mother was coming home that day, and he climbed out of bed. First, he had to find out if Selkie was all right.

He heard the back door open and Cilla's voice call out, "Anyone home?"

"Come on in," his father answered.

Ryan quickly pulled on his clothes and went into the kitchen. Cilla and his father were sitting at the table.

"Why aren't you at work today, Dad?" he asked.

"I figured I had better clean this place before your mother comes home," his father said.

Ryan sat down opposite his father. "Dad, there's something I need to do."

"What's that, Ryan?"

"I need to check on Selkie," Ryan answered. "Please, may I take the dinghy to the island?"

His father looked doubtful. "I'm not sure that's a good idea."

"I'll go with him this time," said Cilla. "And I won't let him do anything stupid."

Ryan frowned at her bossy tone, but his father laughed. "I'm very inclined to believe you, young woman," he said. He looked at Ryan, realizing how important it was for him to know the seal was safe and well. "All right, but I want you to be back before your mother arrives this afternoon. She'll be anxious to see you."

"Thanks, Dad," Ryan sighed with relief. "We'll be careful."

Cilla helped Ryan pack food for Selkie, and together they launched the boat. Ryan became tense and withdrawn as they approached the island. After all he and Selkie had been through, he was fearful for her. She was still very young and quite vulnerable to predators, both on land and in the ocean.

They cruised past the inlet where he and Selkie had sheltered and motored around the base of the island. Ryan leaned forward as the cove came into view. Beach grass swayed in the breeze, and waves lapped the empty shore.

"Selkie!" Ryan called. "Selkie! Where are you?"

"She's not there," said Cilla.

"She's got to be here somewhere." Ryan edged the boat in closer. "She couldn't have left!" He scanned every nook and crevice in the cove. "She can't survive on her own."

"Are you sure?" asked Cilla.

"Of course, I'm sure," he replied. "She needs me. I've got to find her." He revved the engine and the boat spun around, spraying out a foaming jet. Cilla hung on to the rail and bit her lip.

Ryan gunned the boat forward and sped beyond the shelter of the island. He strained his body forward, his eyes searching the ocean ahead.

Cilla saw it first. "Over there." She pointed. "What's that?"

Ryan slowed the boat and edged toward the dark shape. "It's a seal!" he said.

As they came closer, the seal dived. Ryan was silent, waiting for it to resurface.

"Was it her?" asked Cilla. "Was it Selkie?"

"I don't know," he answered. His voice sounded flat, drained of all emotion.

Bubbles rose beside the boat, and a seal's head burst from the water. It looked at them, then glided toward them, stopping a short distance away and resting on the surface.

"My pack!" Ryan rummaged in his backpack and took out his harmonica. He drew the instrument across his mouth, blowing into the reeds. The music floated across the ocean. The seal turned its head, yelped, and swam toward the boat.

When it reached the side, Ryan kneeled down and stretched out his hand. The seal nosed into his palm. "Selkie," he whispered and stroked her head. The seal raised her dark eyes and looked into his.

A series of high-pitched calls sounded from the distance, like seagulls circling a school of fish.

"Look," said Cilla. She pointed to where a group of fur seals leaped and dived in the waves.

Selkie turned her head and spiraled into the water. They saw her surface farther out. Again the seals called their high, yelping greeting. Selkie barked in reply and swam toward them.

Ryan watched as the seals spread out around her then enclosed her in their midst and moved away. He strained to see as the dark shapes became small dots and disappeared from sight.

Cilla touched him gently on the arm. "It's time for us to leave."

Ryan gazed out to sea for a moment longer, then he started the engine and turned the boat toward the mainland. He looked sideways at Cilla.

"You know," he said, "there's an old story my grandmother used to tell about the seals..."

Appendix – Selkie Spellings

The Celtic legend of the selkie grew out of a long tradition of oral storytelling. When people began to write down the story, they used many different spellings for the word "selkie," depending on the dialect of the storyteller. Following are some of the other spellings for the word:

silkie   *selchie*
selky   *silky*

From the Author

The seeds for *Call of the Selkie* were sown when I read the selkie legend to my youngest son, Tony. Seals are intelligent creatures, and some ancient cultures believed they were the link between sea and land. I hope readers of *Call of the Selkie* will gain an appreciation of fur seals and the special relationship that can exist between humans and animals.

I would like to extend special thanks to Bruce Dix for offering me advice and sharing his expert knowledge of fur seals. I would also like to thank my husband, Owen, for his support, and writers Sherryl Jordan and Phyllis Johnston for their friendship and encouragement.

Jean Bennett

From the Illustrator

I was born in Colorado, and have been drawing since I was three. I live with my lovely daughter and scuba buddy, Nicolle, and my son and favorite baseball pal, Paul.

I would like to thank Matt Anderson and Stephanie Walker for modeling for the illustrations in this book, and Megan and Rebecca Anderson for their help with setting up the photographs on which the illustrations are based. I would like to dedicate this book to Daniel Shea, who gave me art, and Elaine Shea, who gave me faith.

Shawn Shea

That's a Laugh
Queen of the Bean
Cinderfella's Big Night
The Flying Pig and the Daredevil Dog
Ants Aren't Antisocial
Charlotte's Web Page
Playing with Words

Thrills and Spills
Mountain Bike Mania
Destination Disaster
Journey to the New World
The Secret of Bunratty Castle
Happy Accidents!
The Chocolate Flier

Challenges and Choices
Call of the Selkie
Trailblazers!
The Hole in the Hill
The Good, the Bad,
　　and Everything Else
On the Edge
The Willow Pattern

Our Wild World
Isn't It Cool? Discovering Antarctica
　　and the Arctic
The Horse, of Course
Trapped by a Teacher
Mystery Bay
The Rain Forest
Feathery Fables

© Text by **Jean Bennett**
© Illustrations by **Shawn Shea**
Edited by **David Nuss**
Designed by **Gary Haney**

© 1999 Shortland Publications, Inc.
All rights reserved. No part of this publication may be reproduced or transmitted in any form or by any means, electronic or mechanical, including photocopying, recording, taping, or any information storage and retrieval system, without permission in writing from the publisher.

04 03 02 01 00
10 9 8 7 6 5 4 3 2

Distributed in the United States by
　RIGBY
　a division of Reed Elsevier Inc.
　P.O. Box 797
　Crystal Lake, IL 60039-0797

Printed in Hong Kong.
ISBN: 1-57257-736-3